Table of contents

Chapter 1: Getting Started with Python

1.1 Introduction to Python: Understanding Python's history and features.

1.2 Setting Up Python: Installing Python and setting up the development environment.

1.3 Your First Python Program: Writing and running a simple "Hello, World!" program.

Chapter 2: Python Basics

2.1 Variables and Data Types: Introducing data types like integers, floats, strings, lists, tuples, and dictionaries.

2.2 Operators: Using arithmetic, assignment, comparison, logical, and other operators.

2.3 Input and Output: Taking user input and displaying output in Python.

Chapter 3: Control Flow and Loops

3.1 Conditional Statements: Using if, else, and elif for decision-making.

3.2 Looping Constructs: Understanding for and while loops for repetitive tasks.

3.3 Break and Continue: Using break and continue statements within loops.

Chapter 4: Functions and Modules

4.1 Defining Functions: Creating functions and passing arguments.

4.2 Function Return Values: Utilizing return statements and handling function outputs.

4.3 Working with Modules: Organizing code and importing functions from modules.

Chapter 5: Object-Oriented Programming in Python

5.1 Introduction to OOP: Understanding the principles of object-oriented programming.

5.2 Classes and Objects: Creating classes, objects, and instance variables.

5.3 Inheritance: Implementing inheritance and using super().

Chapter 6: File Handling and I/O Operations

6.1 Reading Files: Opening and reading text and binary files in Python.

6.2 Writing to Files: Creating, writing, and appending data to files.

6.3 Handling Exceptions: Dealing with errors and exceptions during file operations.

Chapter 7: Working with Libraries and Modules

7.1 Built-in Modules: Exploring useful built-in Python modules like math, random, and datetime.

7.2 Third-Party Libraries: Installing and using external libraries with pip.

Chapter 8: Advanced Data Structures

8.1 Sets and Collections: Working with sets and collections in Python.

8.2 List Comprehensions: Writing concise and efficient code using list comprehensions.

Chapter 9: Python Web Development

9.1 Introduction to Web Frameworks: Exploring Django and Flask.

9.2 Building a Web Application: Creating a simple web app using Python.

Chapter 10: Data Analysis with Python

10.1 Introduction to Data Analysis: Understanding the importance of data analysis.

10.2 NumPy: Performing numerical operations and working with arrays.

10.3 Pandas: Analyzing and manipulating structured data efficiently.

10.4 Data Visualization: Using Matplotlib for data visualization.

Chapter 11: Interacting with Databases

11.1 Connecting to Databases: Working with SQLite, MySQL, or PostgreSQL databases in Python.

11.2 Executing Queries: Executing SQL queries and managing data.

Chapter 12: Introduction to Artificial Intelligence and Machine Learning

12.1 Understanding AI and ML: Overview of AI and machine learning concepts in Python.

12.2 scikit-learn: Utilizing scikit-learn library for basic machine learning tasks.

Chapter 1: Getting Started with Python

1.1 Introduction to Python: Understanding Python's history and features.

Python is a versatile and powerful programming language known for its simplicity and readability. Created by Guido van Rossum and first released in 1991, Python has rapidly gained popularity, becoming one of the most widely used programming languages worldwide. Its design philosophy emphasizes code readability, making it an excellent choice for beginners and experienced developers alike.

Python's History

The origins of Python can be traced back to the late 1980s when Guido van Rossum, a Dutch programmer, started working on a new programming language during his Christmas holidays. He aimed to create a language that was easy to read, efficient, and allowed developers to express their ideas in a clear and concise manner.

The name "Python" was inspired by Guido's love for the British comedy series "Monty Python's Flying Circus." While he wanted a unique and catchy name for the language, he also hoped that it would encourage developers to have fun while coding.

In February 1991, Guido released the first version of Python, known as Python 0.9.0. It included several fundamental features, such as classes with inheritance, exception handling, functions, and modules. Over time, Python evolved through several iterations, with regular updates and enhancements to improve its capabilities and performance.

Key Features of Python

- Readable and Expressive Syntax: Python's syntax is designed to be clear and concise, resembling natural language. This feature allows developers to write code that is easy to read and understand, reducing the chances of errors and enhancing collaboration.
- Cross-Platform Compatibility: Python is a cross-platform language, which means it can run on various operating systems, including Windows, macOS, and Linux. This makes

Python an excellent choice for writing programs that can be deployed on different platforms without major modifications.

- Extensive Standard Library: Python comes with a vast standard library that offers a wide range of modules and packages for various tasks. This library includes functionalities for text processing, network communication, data manipulation, and much more, saving developers time and effort.
- Dynamic Typing and Memory Management: Python is dynamically typed, meaning you don't need to declare variable types explicitly. The interpreter automatically determines the data type at runtime. Additionally, Python manages memory allocation and deallocation, allowing developers to focus on writing code rather than memory management.
- Object-Oriented Programming (OOP): Python supports object-oriented programming, enabling developers to create and use classes and objects. This feature promotes code reusability and organization, making it easier to manage complex projects.
- Community and Ecosystem: Python has a vibrant and supportive community of developers, educators, and enthusiasts. This community contributes to the language's growth, creates numerous libraries,

frameworks, and tools that extend Python's capabilities, and provides extensive documentation and resources for learners.

Python's popularity has been driven by its user-friendly nature, versatility, and widespread adoption in various domains, including web development, data analysis, artificial intelligence, and scientific computing. Whether you are a beginner learning programming for the first time or an experienced developer looking to explore new possibilities, Python offers an inviting and rewarding journey into the world of coding.

1.2 Setting Up Python: Installing Python and setting up the development environment.

Before you can start writing Python code, you need to install Python on your computer and set up a suitable development environment. This chapter will guide you through the process, step by step.

Installing Python

- Check Your System: First, determine whether Python is already installed on your computer. Many modern operating systems come with

Python pre-installed. To check, open a terminal or command prompt and type python --version or python3 --version. If Python is installed, the version number will be displayed.

- Downloading Python: If Python is not installed or you have an older version, visit the official Python website at https://www.python.org/downloads/. Choose the latest stable release suitable for your operating system (Windows, macOS, or Linux) and download the installer.
- Installing Python on Windows:

  o Run the downloaded installer.

  o Check the box to add Python to the system PATH, which allows you to run Python from the command prompt.

  o Click "Install Now" to begin the installation.

  o Once the installation is complete, you can open a command prompt and type python --version to verify the installation.

- Installing Python on macOS:

- Run the downloaded installer.

- Follow the on-screen instructions to complete the installation.

- To verify the installation, open the Terminal and type python3 --version.

- Installing Python on Linux:

  - Python is often pre-installed on Linux systems. To check, open a terminal and type python3 --version.

  - If Python is not installed, use the package manager specific to your distribution (e.g., apt, yum, dnf) to install Python 3.

Setting Up the Development Environment

- Choosing a Text Editor or IDE: Python code can be written using a simple text editor, but using an Integrated Development Environment (IDE) can enhance your productivity. Some popular Python IDEs include:

- o PyCharm: A feature-rich IDE developed specifically for Python.

- o Visual Studio Code (VS Code): A versatile code editor with great Python support through extensions.

- o IDLE: The default Python IDE, available when you install Python.

- Installing a Text Editor or IDE:

  - o Download and install the IDE or text editor of your choice from the official website.

  - o Once installed, launch the IDE or text editor to get started.

- Testing the Setup:

  - o Open your text editor or IDE and create a new Python file with the extension ".py" (e.g., hello.py).

  - o Write a simple Python program, such as:python

  - o print("Hello, Python!")

- Save the file and run it from the command prompt or within the IDE/text editor.

- If you see the output "Hello, Python!" printed, congratulations! Your Python setup is ready to go.

With Python successfully installed and the development environment set up, you're now equipped to dive into the world of Python programming. Whether you're a beginner or an experienced coder, Python's simplicity and versatility make it an excellent language for various applications. Happy coding!

1.3 Your First Python Program: Writing and running a simple "Hello, World!" program.

Now that you have Python installed and your development environment set up, let's write your very first Python program: the classic "Hello, World!" program. This simple program is a tradition in the programming world and serves as an introduction to the language. Follow these steps to create and run your "Hello, World!" program:

- Open Your Text Editor or IDE:

- Launch your chosen text editor or IDE (e.g., Visual Studio Code, PyCharm, IDLE).

- Create a New Python File:

  - In your text editor or IDE, create a new file and save it with the extension ".py" (e.g., hello_world.py). The ".py" extension indicates that this file contains Python code.

- Write the "Hello, World!" Program:

  - In the newly created file, type the following Python code:

  - Python print("Hello, World!"

- Save the File:

  - Save the file after writing the code. Make sure the file is saved in a location where you can easily find it.

- Running the Program:

  - There are two common ways to run your Python program:

- a. Running from the Command Prompt (Terminal):

    o Open the command prompt (Windows) or terminal (macOS/Linux).

    o Navigate to the directory where your hello_world.py file is located using the cd command (e.g., cd Documents/PythonProjects).

    o Once you're in the correct directory, type the following command and press Enter to run the program:

    o python hello_world.py

    o If you're using Python 3, use python3 instead of python in the command:Copy codepython3 hello_world.py

- b. Running from the IDE or Text Editor:

    o Some IDEs and text editors allow you to run Python programs directly from the interface.

    o Look for a "Run" or "Play" button within your IDE or text editor, click it, and your "Hello, World!" program will be executed.

- Observe the Output:

    ○ After running the program, you should see the following output in the command prompt, terminal, or output panel of your IDE/text editor:

    ○ Hello, World!

Congratulations! You've successfully written and run your first Python program. The "Hello, World!" program may seem simple, but it's the first step toward understanding the basics of Python programming. From here, you can explore more complex concepts, create practical applications, and embark on exciting coding projects using Python. Happy coding!

Chapter 2: Python Basics

2.1 Variables and Data Types: Introducing data types like integers, floats, strings, lists, tuples, and dictionaries.

In Python, variables are used to store data, and each variable has a specific data type that determines the kind of data it can hold. Python supports various data types, including integers, floats, strings, lists, tuples, and dictionaries. Let's explore each data type and how to use them:

1. Integers (int):

Integers are whole numbers without a fractional component. You can perform arithmetic operations on integers, such as addition, subtraction, multiplication, and division.

Example:

age = 25

quantity = 10

2. Floats (float):

Floats are numbers with a fractional part, represented by a decimal point. They are used when more precision is required in calculations.

Example:

pi = 3.14159

temperature = 98.6

3. Strings (str):

Strings are sequences of characters, enclosed in single (' ') or double (" ") quotes. They are used to represent text data.

Example:

name = 'John Doe'

address = "123 Main Street"

4. Lists (list):

Lists are ordered collections of items, and they can contain elements of different data types. Lists are mutable, which means you can modify them after creation.

Example:

numbers = [1, 2, 3, 4, 5]

fruits = ['apple', 'orange', 'banana']

mixed_list = [1, 'hello', 3.14, True]

5. Tuples (tuple):

Tuples are similar to lists but are immutable, meaning their elements cannot be changed after creation. They are typically used for fixed collections of items.

Example:

coordinates = (10, 20)

colors = ('red', 'green', 'blue')

6. Dictionaries (dict):

Dictionaries are collections of key-value pairs. Each element in a dictionary is identified by a unique key, and each key is associated with a value. Dictionaries are used to store data in a structured manner for easy retrieval.

Example:

student = {'name': 'Alice', 'age': 21, 'major': 'Computer Science'}

scores = {'math': 95, 'science': 88, 'history': 78}

Type Conversion (Type Casting):

Python allows you to convert variables from one data type to another using type casting functions like int(), float(), str(), list(), and tuple().

Example:

```python
num_str = '25'

num_int = int(num_str)  # Convert the string to an
integer

num_float = float(num_str)  # Convert the string to
a float
```

Understanding data types and how to use them is fundamental to writing effective Python programs. By leveraging the right data types, you can perform various operations, manipulate data, and build more sophisticated applications.

2.2 Operators: Using arithmetic, assignment, comparison, logical, and other operators.

Operators are symbols or special keywords used to perform various operations on variables and values in Python. They enable you to manipulate data, make decisions, and control the flow of your code. Let's explore the most common types of operators in Python:

1. Arithmetic Operators:

Arithmetic operators are used to perform basic mathematical calculations

```python
a = 10

b = 5

# Addition

result_add = a + b  # 15

# Subtraction

result_sub = a - b  # 5

# Multiplication

result_mul = a * b  # 50

# Division

result_div = a / b  # 2.0 (returns a float)

# Floor Division (returns the integer part of the
division)

result_floor_div = a // b  # 2

# Modulo (returns the remainder of the division)

result_mod = a % b  # 0

# Exponentiation
```

result_exp = a ** b # 100000

2. Assignment Operators:

Assignment operators are used to assign values to variables.

x = 10 # Assigns the value 10 to variable x

y = 5   # Assigns the value 5 to variable y

Compound Assignment

x += 2 # Equivalent to x = x + 2 (x becomes 12)

y *= 3 # Equivalent to y = y * 3 (y becomes 15)

3. Comparison Operators:

Comparison operators are used to compare values and return Boolean results (True or False).

a = 10

b = 5

Equal to

is_equal = a == b # False

Not Equal to

is_not_equal = a != b # True

Greater than

is_greater = a > b # True

Less than

is_less = a < b # False

Greater than or Equal to

is_greater_equal = a >= b # True

Less than or Equal to

is_less_equal = a <= b # False

4. Logical Operators:

Logical operators are used to combine Boolean expressions.

p = True

q = False

Logical AND

result_and = p and q # False

```python
# Logical OR

result_or = p or q  # True

# Logical NOT

result_not = not p  # False
```

5. Other Operators:

There are other operators in Python, such as the Membership operators (in and not in) and Identity operators (is and is not).

```python
fruits = ['apple', 'orange', 'banana']

# Membership

is_present = 'apple' in fruits  # True

# Identity

a = 5

b = 5

is_same = a is b  # True
```

Understanding operators is crucial for writing expressive and functional Python code. They allow you to perform calculations, make decisions, and control the behavior of your programs effectively. With this knowledge, you'll be able to create more sophisticated applications and solve complex problems using Python.

2.3 Input and Output: Taking user input and displaying output in Python.

Input and output operations are essential for creating interactive and user-friendly programs in Python. Python provides built-in functions to take user input and display output on the screen. Let's explore how to use these functions:

1. Taking User Input:

To take input from the user, you can use the input() function. The input() function reads a line of text entered by the user and returns it as a string. You can then convert the input to the desired data type if needed.

```python
# Taking user input and storing it in a variable

name = input("Enter your name: ")

print("Hello, " + name + "!")
```

```
# Taking an integer input and converting it to an int

age_str = input("Enter your age: ")

age = int(age_str)

print("You are " + str(age) + " years old.")
```

Note: The input() function always returns a string, so if you need the input as a number, you must explicitly convert it using int(), float(), or other conversion functions.

2. Displaying Output:

To display output on the screen, you can use the print() function. The print() function takes one or more arguments and displays them as text. You can use string concatenation or f-strings to format the output.

```
# Displaying a simple message

print("Hello, World!")

# Displaying variables and formatted output

name = "Alice"

age = 25
```

```python
print("Name: " + name + ", Age: " + str(age))
```

Using f-strings for formatted output (Python 3.6+)

```python
print(f"Name: {name}, Age: {age}")
```

Combining Input and Output:

You can combine user input and output to create interactive programs that respond to user actions.

Interactive program to greet the user

```python
name = input("Enter your name: ")
```

```python
print(f"Hello, {name}!")
```

Calculating the area of a rectangle with user input

```python
length_str = input("Enter the length of the rectangle: ")
```

```python
width_str = input("Enter the width of the rectangle: ")
```

```python
length = float(length_str)
```

```python
width = float(width_str)
```

```python
area = length * width
```

```python
print(f"The area of the rectangle is: {area}")
```

By using input and output operations, you can create programs that engage users and provide meaningful interactions. Whether it's getting user input, displaying results, or responding to user actions, Python's I/O functions make it easy to create dynamic and user-friendly applications.

Chapter 3: Control Flow and Loops

Control Flow and Loops in Python

Control flow and loops are fundamental concepts in programming that allow you to control the flow of your code and perform repetitive tasks. In Python, you can use conditional statements and loops to achieve these functionalities.

1. Conditional Statements:

Conditional statements are used to make decisions in your code based on certain conditions. Python provides three types of conditional statements: if, elif (else if), and else.

If Statement:

```python
age = 25

if age >= 18:

    print("You are an adult.")
```

If-Else Statement:

```python
age = 15

if age >= 18:

    print("You are an adult.")

else:

    print("You are a minor.")
```

If-Elif-Else Statement:

```python
grade = 85

if grade >= 90:

    print("Excellent!")
```

```python
elif grade >= 80:

    print("Good job!")

elif grade >= 70:

    print("Not bad!")

else:

    print("You can do better.")
```

2. Loops:

Loops allow you to execute a block of code repeatedly. Python supports two main types of loops: for loop and while loop.

For Loop:

The for loop is used to iterate over a sequence (e.g., a list, tuple, string) and perform an action on each item.

```python
fruits = ['apple', 'orange', 'banana']

for fruit in fruits:

    print(f"I like {fruit}s.")
```

Range Function with For Loop:

The range() function is often used with the for loop to generate a sequence of numbers.

```
for num in range(1, 6):

    print(num)
```

While Loop:

The while loop is used to repeatedly execute a block of code as long as a specified condition is true.

```
count = 1

while count <= 5:

    print(f"Count: {count}")

    count += 1
```

Break and Continue Statements:

- break: Used to exit the loop prematurely.
- continue: Used to skip the rest of the current iteration and move to the next one.

```
# Break example

for num in range(1, 11):
```

```python
    if num == 5:

        break

    print(num)

# Continue example

for num in range(1, 6):

    if num == 3:

        continue

    print(num)
```

Loops are powerful tools for automating repetitive tasks and processing large amounts of data efficiently.

Python's control flow and loop structures provide the flexibility to make decisions, iterate through data, and create dynamic programs that respond to changing conditions and user inputs. By understanding and utilizing these concepts effectively, you can write more sophisticated and interactive Python programs.

3.1 Conditional Statements: Using if, else, and elif for decision-making.

Conditional statements in Python are used to make decisions based on certain conditions. The primary conditional statements are if, else, and elif (else if). Let's explore how to use these statements for decision-making:

1. if Statement:

The if statement allows you to execute a block of code if a given condition is true.

```
age = 25

if age >= 18:

    print("You are an adult.")
```

2. if-else Statement:

The if-else statement is used to execute different blocks of code based on a condition. If the if condition is true, the code inside the if block is executed. Otherwise, the code inside the else block is executed.

```
age = 15
```

```python
if age >= 18:

    print("You are an adult.")

else:

    print("You are a minor.")
```

3. if-elif-else Statement:

The if-elif-else statement allows you to check multiple conditions and execute different blocks of code accordingly. The elif block(s) are evaluated one by one, and the first one whose condition is true will be executed.

```python
grade = 85

if grade >= 90:

    print("Excellent!")

elif grade >= 80:

    print("Good job!")

elif grade >= 70:

    print("Not bad!")

else:
```

```
    print("You can do better.")
```

In the above example, if the grade is greater than or equal to 90, "Excellent!" will be printed. If not, but grade is greater than or equal to 80, "Good job!" will be printed. If neither of the previous conditions is true, the code inside the else block will be executed.

You can use logical operators (and, or, not) along with conditional statements to create more complex conditions.

```
x = 10

y = 20

if x > 0 and y > 0:

    print("Both x and y are positive.")

elif x > 0 or y > 0:

    print("At least one of x or y is positive.")

else:

    print("Both x and y are non-positive.")
```

Conditional statements are crucial for making decisions in your Python programs. They enable you to control the flow of your code based on various conditions and create dynamic and interactive applications. By using if, else, and elif wisely, you can design programs that respond to different situations and user inputs effectively.

3.2 Looping Constructs in Python: Understanding for and while Loops for Repetitive Tasks

Looping constructs in Python allow you to perform repetitive tasks by executing a block of code multiple times. Python supports two main types of loops: `for` loop and `while` loop. Let's explore each type:

1. for Loop:

The `for` loop is used to iterate over a sequence (e.g., a list, tuple, string) and execute a block of code for each item in the sequence.

```python
fruits = ['apple', 'orange', 'banana']

for fruit in fruits:
    print(f"I like {fruit}s.")
```

Using range() with for Loop:

The `range()` function is often used with the `for` loop to generate a sequence of numbers.

```python
```

```python
for num in range(1, 6):  # Range from 1 to 5 (6 is exclusive)
    print(num)
```

2. while Loop:

The `while` loop is used to repeatedly execute a block of code as long as a specified condition is true.

```python
count = 1

while count <= 5:
    print(f"Count: {count}")
    count += 1
```

In the above example, the code inside the `while` loop will execute as long as the condition `count <= 5` is true. The `count` variable is incremented by 1 in each iteration to ensure the loop eventually terminates.

Using break and continue with Loops:

- `break`: Used to exit the loop prematurely.

- `continue`: Used to skip the rest of the current iteration and move to the next one.

```python
# Break example
for num in range(1, 11):
    if num == 5:
        break
```

```
    print(num)


# Continue example

for num in range(1, 6):

    if num == 3:

        continue

    print(num)
```

In the first example, the loop will break when `num` is equal to 5, and the loop will terminate early. In the second example, the loop will skip printing 3 but continue with the rest of the iterations.

Choosing between for and while Loops:

- Use a `for` loop when you know the number of iterations or when you want to iterate over a specific sequence.

- Use a `while` loop when the number of iterations is uncertain and determined by a specific condition.

Both types of loops are powerful tools for automating repetitive tasks, processing data, and creating efficient and concise Python programs. By choosing the right loop for the task at hand, you can create programs that handle various scenarios and perform tasks with ease.

3.3 Break and Continue: Using break and continue statements within loops.

Break and Continue Statements in Loops: Controlling Loop Execution

In Python, the `break` and `continue` statements are used within loops to control the flow of execution. They allow you to modify the behavior of loops based on specific conditions. Let's explore how to use these statements:

1. Break Statement:

The `break` statement is used to exit a loop prematurely when a certain condition is met. When the `break` statement is encountered within a loop, the loop immediately terminates, and the program execution moves to the next statement after the loop.

```python
# Using break to exit a for loop

for num in range(1, 11):

    if num == 5:

        break

    print(num)
```

In this example, the `for` loop will print numbers from 1 to 4. When `num` becomes 5, the `break` statement is executed, and the loop terminates. As a result, the numbers 6 to 10 are not printed.

2. Continue Statement:

The `continue` statement is used to skip the rest of the current iteration and move on to the next iteration of the loop when a specific condition is met. It allows you to bypass certain code within the loop and continue with the next iteration.

```python
# Using continue to skip an iteration in a for loop

for num in range(1, 6):

    if num == 3:

        continue

    print(num)
```

In this example, the `for` loop will print numbers from 1 to 5. When `num` is 3, the `continue` statement is executed, and the loop proceeds to the next iteration without printing 3.

Common Use Cases:

- Use `break` to exit a loop early when you have found the result you need or when a certain condition is met.

- Use `continue` to skip certain iterations when you want to avoid executing specific code for particular values.

```python
```

```python
# Using break to find the first even number in a list

numbers = [1, 3, 5, 7, 8, 9, 10, 12]

for num in numbers:

    if num % 2 == 0:

        print(f"First even number found: {num}")

        break
```

In this example, the `for` loop iterates through the list of numbers. When it finds the first even number (8), it prints the message and exits the loop with the `break` statement.

Both `break` and `continue` statements are valuable tools for controlling the flow of loop execution and handling specific conditions within loops. By using these statements strategically, you can create more efficient and flexible Python programs.

Chapter 4: Functions and Modules

4.1 Defining Functions: Creating functions and passing arguments.

Functions in Python are reusable blocks of code that perform specific tasks. They help in organizing code, improving reusability, and making programs more modular. You can define your own functions using the `def` keyword. Let's explore how to create functions and pass arguments:

1. Creating Functions:

To define a function, use the `def` keyword followed by the function name and parentheses. The code block inside the function is indented and specifies what the function does.

```python
# Defining a simple function

def greet():

    print("Hello, there!")

# Calling the function

greet()
```

2. Passing Arguments to Functions:

Functions can accept parameters, also known as arguments. Parameters allow you to pass data to the function to work with. You can define parameters inside the parentheses when defining the function.

```python
# Function with parameters

def greet_user(name):

    print(f"Hello, {name}!")

# Calling the function with an argument

greet_user("Alice")
```

3. Default Arguments:

You can also provide default values for function parameters. If a value is not passed for a parameter during the function call, the default value will be used.

```python
# Function with default argument

def greet_with_default(name="User"):
```

```python
    print(f"Hello, {name}!")
```

Calling the function without an argument (uses the default value)

```python
greet_with_default()
```

Calling the function with an argument (overrides the default value)

```python
greet_with_default("Bob")
```
```

### 4. Returning Values:

Functions can return values using the `return` statement. The function can perform calculations and return results to the caller.

```python
# Function with a return statement
def add_numbers(a, b):

    return a + b

# Calling the function and storing the result

result = add_numbers(5, 10)
```
```

```
print("The sum is:", result)
```

5. Multiple Arguments and Keyword Arguments:

Python allows you to pass multiple arguments to functions and use keyword arguments for better readability.

```python
# Function with multiple arguments and keyword arguments

def describe_person(name, age, occupation="Student"):

    print(f"Name: {name}, Age: {age}, Occupation: {occupation}")

# Calling the function with multiple arguments

describe_person("Alice", 25, "Engineer")

# Calling the function using keyword arguments

describe_person(age=30, name="Bob")
```

By defining functions and passing arguments, you can create more flexible and customizable code. Functions help you structure your programs and make them more maintainable and easier to understand. They play a crucial role in building complex applications and solving intricate problems in Python.

4.2 Function Return Values: Utilizing return statements and handling function outputs.

Function Return Values in Python: Utilizing return Statements and Handling Function Outputs

In Python, functions can return values using the `return` statement. The return statement allows a function to compute a result and send it back to the caller. The returned value can then be assigned to a variable or used directly in other parts of the code. Let's explore how to use return statements and handle function outputs:

1. Using Return Statements:

To return a value from a function, use the `return` keyword followed by the value you want to return.

The function will terminate and send the specified value back to the caller.

```python
# Function that returns the sum of two numbers

def add_numbers(a, b):

    return a + b

# Calling the function and storing the result in a variable

result = add_numbers(5, 10)

# Printing the result

print("The sum is:", result)
```

2. Returning Multiple Values:

Python functions can return multiple values as a tuple. The return statement can include multiple values separated by commas.

```python
# Function that returns multiple values
```

```python
def get_user_info():

    name = "Alice"

    age = 25

    occupation = "Engineer"

    return name, age, occupation

# Unpacking the returned tuple into separate variables

name, age, occupation = get_user_info()


# Printing the information

print(f"Name: {name}, Age: {age}, Occupation: {occupation}")
```

3. Handling Function Outputs:

When calling a function that returns a value, you can assign the returned value to a variable for further processing or use it directly in expressions.

```python
```

```python
# Function that checks if a number is even or odd
def is_even(number):
    return number % 2 == 0

# Using the returned value in an if statement
num = 7
if is_even(num):
    print(f"{num} is even.")
else:
    print(f"{num} is odd.")
```

4. Handling None:

If a function does not explicitly return a value, it implicitly returns `None`. It's essential to handle such cases when working with functions.

```python
# Function without a return statement
def greet():
```

```
    print("Hello, there!")

# Calling the function and assigning the return
value to a variable

result = greet()


# Printing the result (it will be None)

print("Result:", result)
```
```

In this case, the `greet()` function does not have a return statement, so it implicitly returns `None`. Be cautious when using the output of functions without return statements.

By understanding return statements and handling function outputs, you can leverage the power of functions to compute results and interact with other parts of your Python code. Functions with return values are useful for performing calculations, retrieving data, and creating reusable components in your programs.
```

4.3 Working with Modules: Organizing code and importing functions from modules.

Modules in Python are files containing Python code that can be reused in different programs. They allow you to organize code, promote reusability, and keep your projects manageable. You can import functions and variables from modules to use them in your current script. Let's explore how to work with modules:

1. Creating a Module:

To create a module, you need to create a Python file with the desired functions and variables. Save the file with a `.py` extension, and it becomes a module that can be imported into other scripts.

mymodule.py:

```python
def greet(name):

    print(f"Hello, {name}!")

def add_numbers(a, b):

    return a + b
```

```python
# Variable in the module

message = "Welcome to my module!"
```

2. Importing Functions and Variables:

To use functions and variables from a module, you need to import them into your current script. You can use the `import` statement to import the entire module or use `from` to import specific functions or variables.

```python
# Import the entire module

import mymodule


# Call functions and access variables from the module

mymodule.greet("Alice")

result = mymodule.add_numbers(5, 10)

print("Result:", result)
```

```python
print(mymodule.message)
```

3. Using Alias:

You can use an alias to provide a shorter or more descriptive name when importing a module.

```python
import mymodule as mm


mm.greet("Bob")
```

4. Importing Specific Functions or Variables:

Instead of importing the entire module, you can import specific functions or variables from the module.

```python
from mymodule import greet, add_numbers
```

```python
greet("Charlie")

result = add_numbers(15, 20)

print("Result:", result)
```

5. Importing Everything from a Module:

You can import all functions and variables from a module using the `*` wildcard. However, it is generally recommended to avoid this practice, as it may lead to name conflicts.

```python
from mymodule import *

greet("Dave")

result = add_numbers(25, 30)

print("Result:", result)
```

By working with modules, you can efficiently organize your code, promote code reusability, and create well-structured Python projects. Importing functions and variables from modules allows you to use external functionalities and extend the capabilities of your scripts with ease. Always choose meaningful names for modules and functions to enhance code readability and maintainability.

Chapter 5: Object-Oriented Programming in Python

5.1 Introduction to OOP: Understanding the principles of object-oriented programming.

Object-Oriented Programming (OOP) is a programming paradigm that focuses on organizing code around objects, which are instances of classes. In Python, everything is an object, and OOP allows you to model real-world entities, abstract data, and interactions more effectively. Here are the key principles and concepts of OOP:

1. Class:

A class is a blueprint for creating objects. It defines a set of attributes (variables) and methods (functions) that represent the characteristics and behaviors of the objects. Classes provide a template for creating instances (objects) with similar properties and actions.

```python
class Car:
```

```python
    # Class attributes

    num_wheels = 4


    # Class method

    def start_engine(self):

        return "Vroom Vroom!"
```

2. Object (Instance):

An object is an instance of a class. It is a concrete representation of the class's attributes and methods. Objects are created based on the class blueprint, and each object has its own unique data.

```python
# Creating instances (objects) of the Car class

car1 = Car()

car2 = Car()
```

3. Encapsulation:

Encapsulation is the principle of bundling data (attributes) and methods (functions) together within a class. It allows objects to hide their internal data from the outside and only expose specific interfaces (methods) for interaction.

4. Abstraction:

Abstraction is the process of simplifying complex systems by focusing on essential properties while hiding unnecessary details. In OOP, classes provide an abstraction layer, allowing you to work with objects using their public interfaces without knowing the underlying implementation.

5. Inheritance:

Inheritance is a mechanism that allows a class (subclass) to inherit properties and behaviors from another class (superclass). Subclasses can extend or override the functionality of the superclass, promoting code reuse and making the code more maintainable.

```python
class ElectricCar(Car):

    # Additional attribute

    battery_capacity = "50 kWh"


    # Overriding the start_engine method

    def start_engine(self):

        return "Silent Mode Activated!"
```

6. Polymorphism:

Polymorphism allows objects of different classes to be treated as if they belong to a common superclass. It enables flexibility and modularity in code, as the same method can work with objects of different types.

```python
def drive(car):

    return car.start_engine()


car1 = Car()

electric_car = ElectricCar()


print(drive(car1))        # Output: "Vroom Vroom!"

print(drive(electric_car)) # Output: "Silent Mode Activated!"

```

By applying the principles of OOP, you can create well-structured, reusable, and maintainable Python code. OOP enables you to model complex systems, design flexible architectures, and implement real-world concepts in your programs effectively. It is a powerful paradigm that encourages modular and object-oriented design practices.

5.2 Classes and Objects: Creating classes, objects, and instance variables.

In Python, classes and objects are fundamental concepts of object-oriented programming. Classes define the blueprint for creating objects, and objects are instances of those classes. Instance variables represent the data unique to each object. Let's explore how to create classes, objects, and instance variables:

1. Creating a Class:

To create a class, use the `class` keyword followed by the class name. Inside the class, you define attributes and methods that represent the characteristics and behaviors of objects.

```python
class Person:

    # Class attribute (shared by all instances)

    species = "Human"


    # Constructor (initialize instance variables)

    def __init__(self, name, age):

        self.name = name

        self.age = age


    # Instance method

    def greet(self):
```

```
    return f"Hello, my name is {self.name} and I
am {self.age} years old."
```

2. Creating Objects (Instances):

To create objects (instances) of a class, you call the class as if it were a function, passing any required arguments to the constructor (`__init__` method). Each object represents a unique instance of the class.

```python
# Creating objects of the Person class

person1 = Person("Alice", 25)

person2 = Person("Bob", 30)
```

3. Instance Variables:

Instance variables are unique to each object. They are defined inside the constructor (`__init__` method) and hold data specific to each object.

```python
# Accessing instance variables
print(person1.name)  # Output: "Alice"
print(person2.age)   # Output: 30
```

4. Instance Methods:

Instance methods are functions defined within the class that can access and manipulate instance variables. They operate on the data associated with a specific object.

```python
# Calling instance methods

print(person1.greet())  # Output: "Hello, my name is Alice and I am 25 years old."

print(person2.greet())  # Output: "Hello, my name is Bob and I am 30 years old."
```

5. Class Attributes vs. Instance Attributes:

Class attributes are shared among all instances of a class and are defined outside the constructor. Instance attributes are unique to each object and are defined inside the constructor.

```python
class MyClass:
```

```python
    class_attr = "Class Attribute"

    def __init__(self, instance_attr):
        self.instance_attr = instance_attr

obj1 = MyClass("Instance Attribute 1")
obj2 = MyClass("Instance Attribute 2")

print(obj1.class_attr)      # Output: "Class Attribute"

print(obj1.instance_attr)   # Output: "Instance Attribute 1"


print(obj2.class_attr)      # Output: "Class Attribute"

print(obj2.instance_attr)   # Output: "Instance Attribute 2"
```

By creating classes, objects, and instance variables, you can model real-world entities and encapsulate data and behavior effectively. Python's object-oriented programming features allow you to build modular and maintainable code, making it easier to manage and extend your projects.

5.3 Inheritance: Implementing inheritance and using super().

Inheritance is a key feature of object-oriented programming that allows a class (subclass) to inherit attributes and methods from another class (superclass). It promotes code reuse and enables you to create hierarchies of classes with increasing levels of specialization. Let's explore how to implement inheritance and use `super()` in Python:

1. Implementing Inheritance:

To create a subclass that inherits from a superclass, you define the subclass with the superclass name in parentheses. The subclass automatically gains access to all attributes and methods of the superclass.

```python
# Superclass (Parent class)

class Animal:

    def __init__(self, name):

        self.name = name


    def make_sound(self):

        return "Generic animal sound"


# Subclass (Child class) inheriting from Animal

class Dog(Animal):

    def __init__(self, name, breed):

        # Call the superclass constructor using super()
```

```
        super().__init__(name)

        self.breed = breed


    def make_sound(self):

        return "Woof!"


    def describe(self):

        return f"I am a {self.breed} dog named
{self.name}."
```
```

### 2. Using super():

In the subclass, you can call the constructor of the superclass using `super()` to initialize the attributes inherited from the superclass.

### 3. Overriding Methods:
```

When a method is defined in both the superclass and subclass, the method in the subclass overrides the one in the superclass. This is called method overriding.

4. Accessing Parent Class Methods:

You can access the methods of the superclass from the subclass using `super()`.

```python
class Cat(Animal):

    def make_sound(self):

        # Call the make_sound method of the superclass

        parent_sound = super().make_sound()

        return f"Meow! But also, {parent_sound}"
```

```
```

5. Multiple Inheritance:

Python supports multiple inheritance, which means a subclass can inherit from multiple superclasses.

```python
class A:

    def method_A(self):

        return "Method A"


class B:

    def method_B(self):

        return "Method B"


# Subclass inheriting from both A and B
```

```
class C(A, B):

    def method_C(self):

        return "Method C"
```
```

```

In this example, class `C` inherits from both classes `A` and `B`, gaining access to the methods defined in both superclasses.

By using inheritance and `super()`, you can create a well-structured class hierarchy, promote code reusability, and build more specialized subclasses. It's important to design your classes carefully, considering their relationships and hierarchies, to achieve a flexible and maintainable codebase.

Chapter 6: File Handling and I/O Operations

6.1 Reading Files: Opening and reading text and binary files in Python.

Python provides built-in functions to open and read files, whether they are text or binary files. Let's explore how to work with files in Python:

1. Opening a Text File:

To open a text file for reading, you can use the `open()` function with the file path and mode "r" (read). The function returns a file object that you can use to read the content of the file.

```python
# Opening a text file for reading

file_path = "example.txt"


try:

    with open(file_path, "r") as file:

        content = file.read()

        print(content)

except FileNotFoundError:

    print("File not found.")
```


2. Reading Text Files:

Once you have opened a text file, you can read its content using various methods such as `read()`, `readline()`, or `readlines()`.

```python
# Using readlines() to read lines as a list of strings

with open(file_path, "r") as file:

    lines = file.readlines()

    for line in lines:

        print(line.strip())  # strip() removes the
newline character at the end

```

3. Opening a Binary File:

To open a binary file for reading, use the `open()` function with mode "rb" (read binary).

```python
# Opening a binary file for reading
binary_file_path = "example.bin"

try:
    with open(binary_file_path, "rb") as binary_file:
        content = binary_file.read()
        print(content)
except FileNotFoundError:
    print("Binary file not found.")
```

4. Reading Binary Files:

Binary files contain non-textual data, such as images, audio, video, etc. When reading binary files, you get the raw bytes from the file, which you can process accordingly.

```python
# Using read() to read binary data (e.g., image file)
with open(binary_file_path, "rb") as binary_file:
    binary_data = binary_file.read()


# Process the binary_data accordingly (e.g., save it
to another file, process it as an image, etc.)
```

5. File Paths and Directories:

When specifying file paths, make sure to provide
the correct file path, including the directory where
the file is located. Python will look for the file in
the current working directory unless you provide an
absolute file path.

To get the current working directory, you can use the `os` module:

```python
import os


current_directory = os.getcwd()

print("Current Working Directory:",
current_directory)
```

Remember to handle file not found or other potential errors when working with files, using appropriate exception handling.

By mastering file handling in Python, you can read and process various types of files, making your programs more versatile and capable of working with different data sources.

6.2 Writing to Files: Creating, writing, and appending data to files.

Python provides built-in functions to create, write, and append data to files. Let's explore how to work with file writing operations:

1. Creating a Text File and Writing Data:

To create a new text file and write data to it, you can use the `open()` function with the file path and mode "w" (write). If the file already exists, it will be overwritten. If the file does not exist, a new file will be created.

```python
# Creating a new text file and writing data to it

file_path = "new_file.txt"
```

```
with open(file_path, "w") as file:

    file.write("Hello, world!\n")

    file.write("This is a new file.\n")
```

2. Appending Data to a Text File:

If you want to add data to an existing text file without overwriting its content, use mode "a" (append) with the `open()` function.

```python
# Appending data to an existing text file

with open(file_path, "a") as file:

    file.write("This is an appended line.\n")
```

3. Writing and Appending Multiple Lines:

You can use loops or lists to write or append multiple lines of data to a text file.

```python
# Writing multiple lines to a text file

lines_to_write = ["Line 1\n", "Line 2\n", "Line 3\n"]


with open(file_path, "w") as file:

    file.writelines(lines_to_write)
```

```python
# Appending multiple lines to an existing text file
```

```
lines_to_append = ["Line 4\n", "Line 5\n", "Line
6\n"]


with open(file_path, "a") as file:

    file.writelines(lines_to_append)
```

4. Writing and Appending Binary Data:

To write or append binary data to a file, use mode
"wb" for writing and "ab" for appending.

```python
# Writing binary data to a file

binary_file_path = "new_binary_file.bin"
```

```python
binary_data_to_write =
b"\x48\x65\x6c\x6c\x6f\x2c\x20\x77\x6f\x72\x6c\x
64\x21"


with open(binary_file_path, "wb") as binary_file:

    binary_file.write(binary_data_to_write)
```


```python
# Appending binary data to an existing file

binary_data_to_append =
b"\x54\x68\x69\x73\x20\x69\x73\x20\x61\x70\x70\
x65\x6e\x64\x65\x64\x20\x6c\x69\x6e\x65\x2e"


with open(binary_file_path, "ab") as binary_file:

    binary_file.write(binary_data_to_append)
```

5. Handling File Writing Errors:

Always handle file writing operations with proper exception handling to deal with potential errors, such as file permission issues or disk space problems.

```python
try:
    with open(file_path, "w") as file:
        # Perform writing operations
except IOError as e:
    print("An error occurred while writing to the file:", e)
```

By mastering file writing operations, you can create, modify, and maintain various types of files in your Python programs, enabling you to store data or generate output in different formats.

6.3 Handling Exceptions: Dealing with errors and exceptions during file operations.

Exception handling is a crucial aspect of file operations in Python. It allows you to gracefully handle errors that may occur during file reading, writing, or other file-related tasks. By using exception handling, you can provide informative error messages and ensure that your program doesn't crash unexpectedly. Let's explore how to deal with errors and exceptions during file operations:

1. Using try-except block:

You can use the try-except block to handle exceptions when performing file operations. The code inside the try block is executed, and if an exception occurs, it's caught by the except block, where you can handle the error.

```python
file_path = "example.txt"


try:

    # Attempt to open and read the file

    with open(file_path, "r") as file:

        content = file.read()

        print(content)

except FileNotFoundError:

    print("File not found.")

except IOError as e:

    print(f"An error occurred while reading the file: {e}")
```


2. Using finally block:

The finally block is optional and is used to define cleanup actions that will be executed regardless of whether an exception occurs or not. It's typically used for releasing resources or performing final operations.

```python
file_path = "example.txt"

try:
    # Attempt to open and read the file
    with open(file_path, "r") as file:
        content = file.read()
        print(content)
except FileNotFoundError:
    print("File not found.")
except IOError as e:
```

```
    print(f"An error occurred while reading the file:
{e}")

finally:

    # Perform cleanup or final operations

    print("File operation completed.")
```

3. Using the Exception Base Class:

You can use the `Exception` base class to catch all types of exceptions. However, it's generally recommended to catch specific exceptions whenever possible to provide more informative error handling.

```python
file_path = "example.txt"
```

```python
try:
    # Attempt to open and read the file
    with open(file_path, "r") as file:
        content = file.read()
        print(content)
except Exception as e:
    print(f"An error occurred: {e}")
```

4. Raising Custom Exceptions:

You can also raise custom exceptions using the `raise` statement when a specific condition is not met. This allows you to create meaningful error messages for specific scenarios in your code.

```python
try:
```

```python
num = int(input("Enter a positive number: "))

if num <= 0:

    raise ValueError("Please enter a positive number.")

except ValueError as ve:

    print(f"Error: {ve}")

```

By properly handling exceptions during file operations, you can enhance the robustness and reliability of your Python programs. Exception handling ensures that your program can gracefully recover from errors, provide useful feedback to users, and continue executing even when unexpected issues occur.

Chapter 7: Working with Libraries and Modules

7.1 Built-in Modules: Exploring useful built-in Python modules like math, random, and datetime.

Python comes with a rich standard library that includes many built-in modules to perform various tasks efficiently. Here are three useful built-in modules: math, random, and datetime.

1. math Module:

The `math` module provides mathematical functions and constants for numerical computations.

Example usage:

```python
import math


# Constants
print(math.pi)      # Output: 3.141592653589793
print(math.e)       # Output: 2.718281828459045
```

```python
# Functions

print(math.sqrt(25))    # Output: 5.0

print(math.sin(math.pi/2))   # Output: 1.0

print(math.cos(math.radians(60)))  # Output: 0.5
```

2. random Module:

The `random` module is used for generating random numbers and making random selections.

Example usage:

```python
import random

# Random integers
```

```python
print(random.randint(1, 100))  # Output: a random integer between 1 and 100


# Random float in the range [0.0, 1.0)
print(random.random())


# Random choice from a sequence
fruits = ["apple", "banana", "orange", "grape"]
print(random.choice(fruits))


# Shuffling a list in-place
random.shuffle(fruits)
print(fruits)
```

3. datetime Module:

The `datetime` module provides classes to work with dates, times, and timedeltas.

Example usage:

```python
import datetime


# Current date and time
current_time = datetime.datetime.now()
print(current_time)


# Creating a specific date
date = datetime.date(2023, 7, 30)
print(date)


# Formatting dates and times
```

```python
formatted_time = current_time.strftime("%Y-%m-%d %H:%M:%S")

print(formatted_time)


# Performing arithmetic with dates and timedeltas

future_date = current_time + datetime.timedelta(days=7)

print(future_date)
```

These built-in modules provide valuable functionalities and save you from implementing common tasks from scratch. By utilizing them effectively, you can improve the efficiency and versatility of your Python programs.

7.2 Third-Party Libraries: Installing and using external libraries with pip.

Third-party libraries in Python extend the capabilities of the language by providing additional functionalities for various tasks. The most common way to install third-party libraries is using `pip`, the package manager for Python. Here's how you can install and use external libraries with pip:

1. Installing a Library with pip:

To install a third-party library, open the terminal or command prompt and run the following command:

```
pip install library_name
```

Replace `library_name` with the name of the library you want to install. For example, to install the popular `requests` library for making HTTP requests, use:

```
pip install requests
```

2. Using a Library in Python:

After installing the library, you can import it into your Python code and use its functionalities.

```python
# Importing the requests library

import requests


# Making an HTTP GET request
```

```
response =
requests.get('https://api.example.com/data')

print(response.status_code)

print(response.json())
```

3. Specifying Library Versions:

You can also specify a specific version of a library
to install using the `==` operator.

```
pip install library_name==1.2.3
```

4. Listing Installed Libraries:

To see a list of all installed libraries and their versions, use the following command:

```
pip list
```

5. Uninstalling a Library:

If you want to remove a library from your Python environment, you can use the `pip uninstall` command.

```
pip uninstall library_name
```

6. Using requirements.txt:

To manage dependencies for your project, you can create a `requirements.txt` file that lists all the libraries and their versions. Then, you can install all the libraries at once using:

```
pip install -r requirements.txt
```

Remember to keep track of the libraries you use in your projects, and consider using virtual environments to isolate project dependencies and prevent conflicts between different projects.

By utilizing third-party libraries with pip, you can leverage the vast Python ecosystem and accelerate your development process by utilizing well-tested and widely-used functionalities created by the community.

Chapter 8: Advanced Data Structures

8.1 Sets and Collections: Working with sets and collections in Python.

Sets and collections are useful data structures in Python for managing collections of elements. Here's a brief overview of sets and collections:

1. Sets:

A set is an unordered collection of unique elements. It is defined using curly braces `{}` or the `set()` constructor.

Example usage:

```python
# Creating a set
fruits = {"apple", "banana", "orange"}
```

```python
print(fruits)  # Output: {'banana', 'orange', 'apple'}


# Adding elements to a set

fruits.add("grape")

print(fruits)  # Output: {'banana', 'orange', 'grape', 'apple'}


# Removing elements from a set

fruits.remove("orange")

print(fruits)  # Output: {'banana', 'grape', 'apple'}


# Checking membership

print("apple" in fruits)  # Output: True


# Set operations

set1 = {1, 2, 3}
set2 = {3, 4, 5}
```

```
union_set = set1.union(set2)

print(union_set)  # Output: {1, 2, 3, 4, 5}


intersection_set = set1.intersection(set2)

print(intersection_set)  # Output: {3}
```

2. Lists, Tuples, and Dictionaries:

Lists, tuples, and dictionaries are built-in collections in Python.

a. Lists:

A list is an ordered collection that allows duplicates and is mutable (can be changed).

Example usage:

```python
# Creating a list
numbers = [1, 2, 3, 4, 5]
print(numbers)


# Adding elements to a list
numbers.append(6)
print(numbers)


# Removing elements from a list
numbers.remove(3)
print(numbers)
```

```python
# Accessing elements in a list
print(numbers[0])  # Output: 1

# Slicing a list
print(numbers[1:4])  # Output: [2, 4, 5]
```

b. Tuples:

A tuple is an ordered collection that allows duplicates and is immutable (cannot be changed).

Example usage:

```python
# Creating a tuple
colors = ("red", "green", "blue")
```

```
print(colors)
```

```
# Accessing elements in a tuple
print(colors[0])  # Output: "red"
```

c. Dictionaries:

A dictionary is an unordered collection of key-value pairs, where each key must be unique.

Example usage:

```python
# Creating a dictionary
person = {"name": "Alice", "age": 30,
"occupation": "Engineer"}
```

```python
print(person)


# Accessing values in a dictionary
print(person["name"])  # Output: "Alice"
print(person.get("age"))  # Output: 30


# Modifying values in a dictionary
person["age"] = 35
print(person)


# Adding new key-value pairs to a dictionary
person["city"] = "New York"
print(person)


# Removing key-value pairs from a dictionary
del person["occupation"]
```

```
print(person)
```

3. Collections module:

The `collections` module in Python provides specialized data structures like `namedtuple`, `defaultdict`, and `Counter`, which can be very helpful for certain tasks.

```python
from collections import namedtuple, defaultdict, Counter

# namedtuple
Point = namedtuple('Point', ['x', 'y'])
p = Point(1, 2)
print(p.x, p.y)  # Output: 1 2
```

```python
# defaultdict

# Automatically initializes new keys with a default value

fruit_counts = defaultdict(int)

fruit_counts['apple'] += 1

fruit_counts['banana'] += 1

print(fruit_counts)  # Output: defaultdict(<class 'int'>, {'apple': 1, 'banana': 1})


# Counter

# Counts occurrences of elements in a collection

fruits = ['apple', 'banana', 'apple', 'orange', 'banana', 'apple']

fruit_counter = Counter(fruits)

print(fruit_counter)  # Output: Counter({'apple': 3, 'banana': 2, 'orange': 1})

```
```
```

Using sets and collections in Python allows you to manage and manipulate data efficiently and effectively. Each data structure serves different purposes, and understanding their characteristics can help you choose the right one for your specific use case.

8.2 List Comprehensions: Writing concise and efficient code using list comprehensions.

List comprehensions are a concise and efficient way to create lists in Python. They allow you to generate lists based on some logic or transformation in a single line of code. List comprehensions are often preferred over traditional for-loops for their readability and performance. Here's how to use list comprehensions:

1. Basic List Comprehension:

The basic syntax of a list comprehension is as follows:

```python
new_list = [expression for item in iterable]
```

Example:

```python
# Traditional for-loop to generate a list of squares
numbers = [1, 2, 3, 4, 5]
squares = []
for num in numbers:
    squares.append(num ** 2)
print(squares)  # Output: [1, 4, 9, 16, 25]

# Using list comprehension
```

```python
numbers = [1, 2, 3, 4, 5]
squares = [num ** 2 for num in numbers]
print(squares)  # Output: [1, 4, 9, 16, 25]
```

2. Conditional List Comprehension:

You can include a conditional statement in the list comprehension to filter elements based on a certain condition.

```python
# Traditional for-loop to filter even numbers
numbers = [1, 2, 3, 4, 5, 6, 7, 8, 9, 10]
even_numbers = []
for num in numbers:
    if num % 2 == 0:
```

```python
        even_numbers.append(num)

print(even_numbers)  # Output: [2, 4, 6, 8, 10]


# Using list comprehension with a conditional statement

numbers = [1, 2, 3, 4, 5, 6, 7, 8, 9, 10]

even_numbers = [num for num in numbers if num % 2 == 0]

print(even_numbers)  # Output: [2, 4, 6, 8, 10]
```

3. Nested List Comprehension:

You can use nested list comprehensions to create more complex lists.

```python
# Traditional for-loop to create a matrix
```

```python
matrix = []
for i in range(3):
    row = []
    for j in range(3):
        row.append(i * j)
    matrix.append(row)
print(matrix)  # Output: [[0, 0, 0], [0, 1, 2], [0, 2, 4]]


# Using nested list comprehension
matrix = [[i * j for j in range(3)] for i in range(3)]
print(matrix)  # Output: [[0, 0, 0], [0, 1, 2], [0, 2, 4]]
```

4. Set and Dictionary Comprehensions:

List comprehensions can be adapted to create sets and dictionaries as well.

```python
# Set comprehension
numbers = [1, 2, 3, 4, 5]
squares_set = {num ** 2 for num in numbers}
print(squares_set)  # Output: {1, 4, 9, 16, 25}


# Dictionary comprehension
fruits = ["apple", "banana", "orange"]
fruit_lengths = {fruit: len(fruit) for fruit in fruits}
print(fruit_lengths)  # Output: {'apple': 5, 'banana': 6, 'orange': 6}
```

List comprehensions allow you to write more concise and readable code while maintaining good performance. They are a powerful tool in Python for creating lists, sets, and dictionaries with ease. However, be mindful of using them excessively in a single line, as it might decrease code readability. Use list comprehensions judiciously to improve code quality and efficiency.

Chapter 9: Python Web Development

9.1 Introduction to Web Frameworks: Exploring Django and Flask.

Web frameworks are essential tools for building web applications in Python. They provide a set of pre-built components and tools that simplify the development process, making it faster and more efficient. Two popular Python web frameworks are Django and Flask:

Django:

Django is a high-level, full-featured web framework that follows the "batteries-included" philosophy. It comes with many built-in features, including an ORM (Object-Relational Mapping) for database management, authentication system, admin interface, and more. Django is designed to encourage rapid development and follows the Model-View-Template (MVT) architectural pattern.

Key features of Django:

- Robust ORM for database interactions (supporting various database backends).

- Authentication system with user management and permissions.

- Admin interface for managing application data.

- URL routing and views for handling user requests and rendering responses.

- Template engine for creating HTML templates with dynamic content.

- Built-in security features, such as CSRF protection and SQL injection prevention.

Django is well-suited for large and complex web applications, and it's widely used by many big organizations and startups.

Flask:

Flask, on the other hand, is a lightweight and flexible web framework that follows the "micro" philosophy. It provides the essentials for web development without imposing a particular project structure or dependencies. Flask is designed to be simple, extensible, and easy to learn, making it a popular choice for small to medium-sized applications or APIs.

Key features of Flask:

- Simple routing system for defining URL patterns and view functions.

- Jinja2 template engine for creating dynamic HTML templates.

- Minimal and modular design, allowing developers to use extensions as needed.

- No built-in ORM or authentication system, but can be easily integrated with third-party libraries.

- Customizable and suitable for building APIs, microservices, and simple web applications.

Flask's lightweight nature makes it a good choice for projects that require more customization and don't need all the features provided by a full-stack framework like Django.

Both Django and Flask have active and supportive communities, with extensive documentation and a wide range of third-party libraries and extensions. The choice between the two frameworks depends on the project requirements, complexity, and developer preferences. Django is ideal for large and feature-rich applications, while Flask is well-suited for smaller projects and those seeking more control over the application structure.

9.2 Building a Web Application: Creating a simple web app using Python.

To build a simple web application using Python, we will use the Flask web framework. Flask allows us to create a basic web application with just a few lines of code. In this example, we'll create a web app that displays a "Hello, World!" message.

Here's a step-by-step guide to building the web application:

Step 1: Install Flask

Make sure you have Flask installed. If not, you can install it using `pip`:

```
pip install Flask
```

Step 2: Create the App

Create a new Python file (e.g., `app.py`) and import the necessary modules:

```python
from flask import Flask
```

Step 3: Create the Flask App Instance

Instantiate the Flask application and create a route for the home page:

```python
app = Flask(__name__)


@app.route('/')

def home():

    return 'Hello, World!'

```

Step 4: Run the App

Add the following code at the end of the `app.py` file to run the application:

```python
if __name__ == '__main__':
    app.run()
```

Step 5: Run the Web Application

Open a terminal or command prompt, navigate to the directory where `app.py` is located, and run the following command:

```
python app.py
```

The Flask development server will start running. You should see an output similar to:

```
```

* Running on http://127.0.0.1:5000/ (Press CTRL+C to quit)

```
```

Step 6: Access the Web Application

Open your web browser and go to `http://127.0.0.1:5000/`. You should see the "Hello, World!" message displayed on the page.

That's it! You have created a simple web application using Python and Flask. Of course, this is just a basic example, but you can extend it further by adding more routes, templates, and functionalities as needed. Flask provides many features and extensions to build more complex web applications, such as handling forms, connecting to databases, and serving static files.

Chapter 10: Data Analysis with Python

10.1 Introduction to Data Analysis:
Understanding the importance of data analysis.

Data analysis is a crucial process in extracting valuable insights and knowledge from raw data. It involves examining, cleaning, transforming, and interpreting data to make informed decisions and support business strategies. Data analysis plays a fundamental role in various domains, from scientific research and finance to marketing and healthcare. Here are some key reasons why data analysis is important:

1. Data-Driven Decision Making:

Data analysis allows organizations to make data-driven decisions. By analyzing historical and real-time data, businesses can identify patterns, trends, and correlations to guide their strategies and operations. Data-driven decisions reduce guesswork and lead to more effective and efficient outcomes.

2. Identifying Business Opportunities:

Through data analysis, businesses can identify potential opportunities for growth and improvement. Analyzing customer behavior, market trends, and competitor performance can help organizations stay ahead of the competition and capitalize on emerging opportunities.

3. Improving Performance and Efficiency:

Data analysis can uncover inefficiencies and bottlenecks in processes, allowing organizations to optimize their operations for improved performance. By identifying areas that need improvement, businesses can streamline workflows and reduce costs.

4. Personalization and Customer Experience:

Data analysis enables organizations to understand customer preferences and behavior better. With this knowledge, businesses can personalize their products and services, leading to enhanced customer experiences and increased customer loyalty.

5. Risk Assessment and Mitigation:

Data analysis plays a critical role in risk assessment and management. By analyzing historical data and patterns, businesses can identify potential risks and take preventive measures to mitigate them effectively.

6. Research and Scientific Advancements:

In scientific research, data analysis is fundamental to drawing conclusions and making discoveries. It helps researchers validate hypotheses, analyze experimental results, and draw meaningful conclusions.

7. Public Health and Healthcare:

In the healthcare industry, data analysis is essential for disease tracking, patient outcomes assessment, and identifying health trends. Data analysis can help healthcare professionals make informed decisions and improve patient care.

8. Real-Time Monitoring and Predictive Analytics:

Data analysis enables real-time monitoring of systems and processes. It also supports predictive analytics, where historical data is used to predict future events and trends, enabling proactive decision-making.

9. Government and Policy Making:

Governments use data analysis to make informed policy decisions, allocate resources efficiently, and measure the effectiveness of their programs and initiatives.

In summary, data analysis empowers organizations and individuals to make informed decisions, optimize performance, and uncover valuable insights. It has become an integral part of various industries, helping businesses stay competitive, scientists make discoveries, and governments govern effectively. As data continues to grow in volume and complexity, data analysis will remain a vital skill for extracting knowledge from this vast resource.

10.2 NumPy: Performing numerical operations and working with arrays.

NumPy is a powerful Python library for numerical operations and working with arrays. It provides efficient and convenient array manipulation functionalities, making it a fundamental tool for scientific computing and data analysis. Here's an introduction to using NumPy for numerical operations and array manipulation:

1. Installing NumPy:

Before using NumPy, you need to install it. You can install NumPy using `pip`:

```
pip install numpy
```

2. Importing NumPy:

To start using NumPy in your Python code, you need to import it:

```python
import numpy as np
```

3. Creating NumPy Arrays:

NumPy arrays are the core data structure for performing numerical operations. You can create arrays using `np.array()` or other NumPy functions like `np.zeros()`, `np.ones()`, and `np.arange()`.

```python
# Creating a 1D array
arr1d = np.array([1, 2, 3, 4, 5])
print(arr1d)  # Output: [1 2 3 4 5]
```

```python
# Creating a 2D array
arr2d = np.array([[1, 2, 3], [4, 5, 6]])
print(arr2d)
# Output:
# [[1 2 3]
#  [4 5 6]]


# Creating an array of zeros
zeros_arr = np.zeros(5)
print(zeros_arr)  # Output: [0. 0. 0. 0. 0.]


# Creating an array of ones
ones_arr = np.ones((2, 3))
print(ones_arr)
# Output:
# [[1. 1. 1.]
```

```python
#  [1. 1. 1.]]
```

```python
# Creating a range of values
range_arr = np.arange(0, 10, 2)
print(range_arr)  # Output: [0 2 4 6 8]
```

4. Basic Numerical Operations:

You can perform basic numerical operations on NumPy arrays, including element-wise operations, scalar operations, and aggregations.

```python
# Element-wise operations
arr1 = np.array([1, 2, 3])
arr2 = np.array([4, 5, 6])
add_result = arr1 + arr2
```

```python
print(add_result)  # Output: [5 7 9]

# Scalar operations
scalar_mult = arr1 * 2
print(scalar_mult)  # Output: [2 4 6]

# Aggregations
sum_result = np.sum(arr1)
print(sum_result)  # Output: 6

max_value = np.max(arr2)
print(max_value)  # Output: 6
```

5. Indexing and Slicing:

You can access elements and perform slicing on NumPy arrays similar to Python lists.

```python
arr = np.array([10, 20, 30, 40, 50])

# Accessing elements
print(arr[0])  # Output: 10
print(arr[-1])  # Output: 50

# Slicing
print(arr[1:4])  # Output: [20 30]
```

6. Broadcasting:

NumPy allows broadcasting, which enables element-wise operations on arrays with different shapes.

```python
arr = np.array([[1, 2, 3], [4, 5, 6]])
scalar = 10


result = arr + scalar
print(result)
# Output:
# [[11 12 13]
#  [14 15 16]]
```

NumPy provides a vast array of functionalities for numerical operations, linear algebra, statistics, and more. It forms the foundation for many other scientific Python libraries and is widely used in data analysis, machine learning, and computational science. Mastering NumPy is essential for any Python programmer working with numerical data and scientific computing tasks.

10.3 Pandas: Analyzing and manipulating structured data efficiently.

Pandas is a powerful Python library widely used for data manipulation and analysis. It provides easy-to-use data structures and functions to handle structured data efficiently, making it an essential tool for data scientists and analysts. Here's an introduction to Pandas and its capabilities for data analysis and manipulation:

1. Installing Pandas:

Before using Pandas, you need to install it. You can install Pandas using `pip`:

```
pip install pandas
```

2. Importing Pandas:

To start using Pandas in your Python code, you need to import it:

```python
import pandas as pd
```

3. Pandas Data Structures:

Pandas provides two main data structures: Series and DataFrame.

Series:

A Series is a one-dimensional labeled array, similar to a Python list. It can hold data of any type, including integers, floats, strings, and more. A Series also has a labeled index, which allows for easy and efficient data access.

```python
```

```python
# Creating a Series
s = pd.Series([10, 20, 30, 40, 50])
print(s)
# Output:
# 0    10
# 1    20
# 2    30
# 3    40
# 4    50
# dtype: int64


# Accessing elements in the Series
print(s[2])  # Output: 30
```

DataFrame:

A DataFrame is a two-dimensional labeled data structure, similar to a spreadsheet or SQL table. It consists of rows and columns, where each column can contain data of different types. DataFrames are particularly useful for handling structured data like CSV files or database tables.

```python
# Creating a DataFrame from a dictionary
data = {
    'Name': ['Alice', 'Bob', 'Charlie'],
    'Age': [25, 30, 35],
    'City': ['New York', 'London', 'Tokyo']
}
df = pd.DataFrame(data)
print(df)
# Output:
#     Name  Age     City
# 0  Alice   25  New York
```

```
# 1     Bob   30    London
# 2   Charlie  35    Tokyo

# Accessing columns in the DataFrame
print(df['Name'])
# Output:
# 0     Alice
# 1       Bob
# 2   Charlie
# Name: Name, dtype: object

# Accessing rows in the DataFrame using loc
print(df.loc[1])
# Output:
# Name      Bob
# Age        30
```

```
# City    London
# Name: 1, dtype: object
```

4. Data Manipulation with Pandas:

Pandas offers various functions for data manipulation, including filtering, grouping, sorting, and merging data.

```python
# Filtering data
young_people = df[df['Age'] < 30]
print(young_people)
# Output:
#    Name  Age    City
# 0  Alice  25  New York
```

```python
# Grouping data and calculating statistics
grouped_city = df.groupby('City').mean()
print(grouped_city)
# Output:
#         Age
# City
# London    30
# New York  25
# Tokyo     35


# Sorting data
sorted_df = df.sort_values(by='Age',
ascending=False)
print(sorted_df)
# Output:
#     Name  Age    City
# 2  Charlie  35    Tokyo
```

```
# 1     Bob   30   London

# 0   Alice  25  New York


# Merging DataFrames

data1 = {'ID': [1, 2, 3], 'Grade': ['A', 'B', 'C']}

data2 = {'ID': [2, 3, 4], 'Marks': [90, 85, 95]}

df1 = pd.DataFrame(data1)

df2 = pd.DataFrame(data2)

merged_df = pd.merge(df1, df2, on='ID', how='inner')

print(merged_df)

# Output:

#   ID Grade  Marks

# 0 2    B    90

# 1 3    C    85

```
```
```

5. Handling Missing Data:

Pandas provides functions to handle missing data, like filling missing values or dropping rows with missing data.

```python
# Handling missing data
data = {'A': [1, 2, None, 4], 'B': [5, None, 7, 8]}
df = pd.DataFrame(data)
print(df)
# Output:
#    A    B
# 0  1.0  5.0
# 1  2.0  NaN
# 2  NaN  7.0
# 3  4.0  8.0
```

```python
# Filling missing values with a specified value

df_filled = df.fillna(0)

print(df_filled)

# Output:

#    A   B

# 0
```

10.4 Data Visualization: Using Matplotlib for data visualization.

Matplotlib is a popular Python library for creating various types of plots and visualizations. It provides a wide range of functionalities to represent data effectively, making it an essential tool for data analysts and scientists. Here's an introduction to using Matplotlib for data visualization:

1. Installing Matplotlib:

Before using Matplotlib, you need to install it. You can install Matplotlib using `pip`:

```
pip install matplotlib
```

2. Importing Matplotlib:

To start using Matplotlib in your Python code, you need to import it:

```python
import matplotlib.pyplot as plt
```

3. Creating Basic Plots:

Matplotlib provides various plot types, including line plots, scatter plots, bar plots, and more. Here are some examples of basic plots:

Line Plot:

```python
# Line Plot
x = [1, 2, 3, 4, 5]
y = [10, 15, 20, 25, 30]
plt.plot(x, y)
plt.xlabel('X-axis')
plt.ylabel('Y-axis')
plt.title('Line Plot')
plt.show()
```

Scatter Plot:

```python
# Scatter Plot
x = [1, 2, 3, 4, 5]
y = [10, 15, 20, 25, 30]
plt.scatter(x, y)
plt.xlabel('X-axis')
plt.ylabel('Y-axis')
plt.title('Scatter Plot')
plt.show()
```

Bar Plot:

```python
# Bar Plot
x = ['A', 'B', 'C', 'D', 'E']
```

```python
y = [10, 15, 20, 25, 30]
plt.bar(x, y)
plt.xlabel('X-axis')
plt.ylabel('Y-axis')
plt.title('Bar Plot')
plt.show()
```

4. Customizing Plots:

You can customize the appearance of plots by adding labels, legends, gridlines, and more:

```python
# Customizing plots
x = [1, 2, 3, 4, 5]
y1 = [10, 15, 20, 25, 30]
y2 = [5, 10, 15, 20, 25]
```

```
plt.plot(x, y1, label='Line 1')

plt.plot(x, y2, label='Line 2')


plt.xlabel('X-axis')

plt.ylabel('Y-axis')

plt.title('Customized Line Plot')

plt.legend()  # Show legend

plt.grid(True)  # Show gridlines

plt.show()
```

5. Subplots:

You can create multiple plots in one figure using subplots:

```python
```

```python
# Subplots

x = [1, 2, 3, 4, 5]

y1 = [10, 15, 20, 25, 30]

y2 = [5, 10, 15, 20, 25]


fig, (ax1, ax2) = plt.subplots(2, 1)


ax1.plot(x, y1)

ax1.set_ylabel('Y1-axis')

ax1.set_title('Subplot 1')


ax2.plot(x, y2)

ax2.set_xlabel('X-axis')

ax2.set_ylabel('Y2-axis')

ax2.set_title('Subplot 2')
```

```python
plt.tight_layout()

plt.show()
```


6. Saving Plots:

You can save plots to files in various formats, such as PNG, JPEG, PDF, or SVG:


```python
# Save plot to a file

x = [1, 2, 3, 4, 5]

y = [10, 15, 20, 25, 30]


plt.plot(x, y)

plt.xlabel('X-axis')

plt.ylabel('Y-axis')

plt.title('Line Plot')
```

```
plt.savefig('line_plot.png')
```

```
```

Matplotlib is a versatile library that allows you to create complex visualizations and plots to represent data effectively. With its extensive customization options and support for various plot types, Matplotlib is an indispensable tool for data visualization in Python.

Chapter 11: Interacting with Databases

11.1 Connecting to Databases: Working with SQLite, MySQL, or PostgreSQL databases in Python.

In Python, you can connect to SQLite, MySQL, or PostgreSQL databases using different libraries. Here's an overview of how to work with each database in Python:

1. SQLite:

SQLite is a lightweight, serverless, and self-contained database engine that is easy to use and perfect for small to medium-sized applications or testing purposes. Python includes built-in support for SQLite, so you don't need to install any additional libraries.

To work with SQLite in Python, you can use the `sqlite3` module:

```python
import sqlite3

# Connect to a SQLite database or create one if it
doesn't exist

conn = sqlite3.connect('database.db')

# Create a cursor object to interact with the
database

cursor = conn.cursor()

# Execute SQL queries
cursor.execute('CREATE TABLE IF NOT EXISTS
users (id INTEGER PRIMARY KEY, name TEXT,
age INTEGER)')

cursor.execute('INSERT INTO users (name, age)
VALUES (?, ?)', ('Alice', 30))

cursor.execute('SELECT * FROM users')

rows = cursor.fetchall()
```

```
# Commit changes and close the connection
conn.commit()
conn.close()
```

2. MySQL:

To work with MySQL databases, you can use the `mysql-connector-python` library. Before using it, you need to install it using `pip`:

```
pip install mysql-connector-python
```

```python
import mysql.connector
```

```python
# Connect to the MySQL database
conn = mysql.connector.connect(
    host='localhost',
    user='username',
    password='password',
    database='database_name'
)


# Create a cursor object to interact with the
database
cursor = conn.cursor()


# Execute SQL queries
cursor.execute('CREATE TABLE IF NOT EXISTS
users (id INT AUTO_INCREMENT PRIMARY
KEY, name VARCHAR(255), age INT)')
```

```
cursor.execute('INSERT INTO users (name, age)
VALUES (%s, %s)', ('Bob', 25))

cursor.execute('SELECT * FROM users')

rows = cursor.fetchall()


# Commit changes and close the connection

conn.commit()

conn.close()
```

3. PostgreSQL:

To work with PostgreSQL databases, you can use
the `psycopg2` library. Before using it, you need to
install it using `pip`:

```
pip install psycopg2
```

```python
import psycopg2

# Connect to the PostgreSQL database
conn = psycopg2.connect(
    host='localhost',
    user='username',
    password='password',
    database='database_name'
)

# Create a cursor object to interact with the database
cursor = conn.cursor()

# Execute SQL queries
```

```python
cursor.execute('CREATE TABLE IF NOT EXISTS
users (id SERIAL PRIMARY KEY, name
VARCHAR(255), age INT)')

cursor.execute('INSERT INTO users (name, age)
VALUES (%s, %s)', ('Charlie', 35))

cursor.execute('SELECT * FROM users')

rows = cursor.fetchall()


# Commit changes and close the connection

conn.commit()

conn.close()
```
```

Remember to replace `username`, `password`, and
`database_name` with your actual database
credentials and name.


Each database has its strengths and use cases, so
choose the one that best fits your project
```

requirements. Whichever database you choose, Python provides libraries to work seamlessly with them and perform various database operations.

11.2 Executing Queries: Executing SQL queries and managing data.

To execute SQL queries and manage data in Python, you can use the appropriate database library, such as `sqlite3` for SQLite, `mysql-connector-python` for MySQL, or `psycopg2` for PostgreSQL. Here's an overview of how to execute SQL queries and manage data in each database using Python:

1. SQLite:

SQLite is a serverless database engine, and Python has built-in support for it with the `sqlite3` module.


```python
import sqlite3
```

```python
# Connect to the SQLite database or create one if it
doesn't exist

conn = sqlite3.connect('database.db')


# Create a cursor object to interact with the
database

cursor = conn.cursor()


# Execute SQL queries

cursor.execute('CREATE TABLE IF NOT EXISTS
users (id INTEGER PRIMARY KEY, name TEXT,
age INTEGER)')

cursor.execute('INSERT INTO users (name, age)
VALUES (?, ?)', ('Alice', 30))

cursor.execute('SELECT * FROM users')

rows = cursor.fetchall()
```

```python
# Commit changes and close the connection
conn.commit()
conn.close()
```

2. MySQL:

To work with MySQL databases, you need to install the `mysql-connector-python` library.

```python
import mysql.connector

# Connect to the MySQL database
conn = mysql.connector.connect(
    host='localhost',
    user='username',
    password='password',
```

```python
    database='database_name'
)


# Create a cursor object to interact with the
database

cursor = conn.cursor()


# Execute SQL queries

cursor.execute('CREATE TABLE IF NOT EXISTS
users (id INT AUTO_INCREMENT PRIMARY
KEY, name VARCHAR(255), age INT)')

cursor.execute('INSERT INTO users (name, age)
VALUES (%s, %s)', ('Bob', 25))

cursor.execute('SELECT * FROM users')

rows = cursor.fetchall()


# Commit changes and close the connection

conn.commit()
```

```
conn.close()
```

3. PostgreSQL:

To work with PostgreSQL databases, you need to install the `psycopg2` library.

```python
import psycopg2

# Connect to the PostgreSQL database
conn = psycopg2.connect(
    host='localhost',
    user='username',
    password='password',
    database='database_name'
)
```

```python
# Create a cursor object to interact with the
database

cursor = conn.cursor()


# Execute SQL queries

cursor.execute('CREATE TABLE IF NOT EXISTS
users (id SERIAL PRIMARY KEY, name
VARCHAR(255), age INT)')

cursor.execute('INSERT INTO users (name, age)
VALUES (%s, %s)', ('Charlie', 35))

cursor.execute('SELECT * FROM users')

rows = cursor.fetchall()


# Commit changes and close the connection

conn.commit()

conn.close()
```
```
```

Remember to replace `username`, `password`, and `database_name` with your actual database credentials and name.

After connecting to the database and executing the queries, you can use the `fetchall()`, `fetchone()`, or other appropriate methods of the cursor object to retrieve the query results. The `commit()` method is used to save changes to the database, and the `close()` method is used to close the database connection.

By using the appropriate database library and Python's capabilities, you can effectively execute SQL queries and manage data in your chosen database system.

Chapter 12: Introduction to Artificial Intelligence and Machine Learning

12.1 Understanding AI and ML: Overview of AI and machine learning concepts in Python.

AI (Artificial Intelligence) and ML (Machine Learning) are two interconnected fields that involve the development of intelligent systems capable of performing tasks that typically require human intelligence. Python has become a prominent language in both AI and ML due to its versatility, extensive libraries, and ease of use. Here's an overview of AI and machine learning concepts in Python:

Artificial Intelligence (AI):

AI encompasses the development of computer systems that can simulate human intelligence. It includes various subfields, such as machine learning, natural language processing, computer vision, robotics, and more. Key concepts in AI include:

1. **Machine Learning (ML)**: A subset of AI focused on enabling computers to learn from data and improve performance over time without being explicitly programmed.

2. **Natural Language Processing (NLP)**: The ability of machines to understand, interpret, and generate human language.

3. **Computer Vision**: AI algorithms that enable machines to interpret and understand visual information from images or videos.

4. **Robotics**: The development of intelligent machines that can interact with the physical world and perform tasks autonomously.

Machine Learning (ML):

ML is a crucial aspect of AI that involves the use of algorithms and statistical models to enable computers to learn patterns from data and make predictions or decisions without explicit programming. In Python, there are various libraries for ML, such as:

1. **Scikit-learn**: A comprehensive library for various ML algorithms, including classification, regression, clustering, and more.

2. **TensorFlow**: Developed by Google, TensorFlow is an open-source ML framework known for its flexibility and scalability.

3. **Keras**: Built on top of TensorFlow, Keras provides a user-friendly API for deep learning models.

4. **PyTorch**: Another popular deep learning library known for its dynamic computation graph and ease of use.

ML Concepts in Python:

Here are some fundamental ML concepts commonly used in Python:

1. **Data Preprocessing**: Cleaning, transforming, and preparing data for training ML models.

2. **Supervised Learning**: Training ML models with labeled data for tasks like classification and regression.

3. **Unsupervised Learning**: Training models with unlabeled data for clustering or dimensionality reduction.

4. **Cross-Validation**: Evaluating ML models to avoid overfitting and assess performance on unseen data.

5. **Model Evaluation Metrics**: Metrics like accuracy, precision, recall, and F1-score to assess model performance.

6. **Hyperparameter Tuning**: Adjusting model hyperparameters to optimize performance.

7. **Feature Engineering**: Selecting and creating relevant features from data to improve model performance.

8. **Model Deployment**: Making ML models usable in real-world applications.

Python's rich ecosystem of libraries and frameworks, along with its simplicity, makes it an excellent choice for AI and ML projects. Whether it's for building sophisticated deep learning models or simple ML pipelines, Python offers the tools needed to explore and implement AI and ML solutions effectively.

12.2 scikit-learn: Utilizing scikit-learn library for basic machine learning tasks.

Scikit-learn is a popular and versatile machine learning library in Python that provides a wide range of tools for various machine learning tasks. It is built on top of other scientific Python libraries, such as NumPy, SciPy, and matplotlib, making it an excellent choice for data analysis and machine learning projects. Here's an overview of how to utilize scikit-learn for basic machine learning tasks:

1. Installing scikit-learn:

Before using scikit-learn, you need to install it. You can install scikit-learn using `pip`:

```
pip install scikit-learn
```

```
```

2. Importing scikit-learn:

To start using scikit-learn in your Python code, you need to import it:

```python
import sklearn
```

3. Basic Machine Learning Tasks:

a. Data Loading and Preprocessing:

Scikit-learn provides functions to load sample datasets for practice and real-world datasets. It also includes tools for data preprocessing.

```python
from sklearn.datasets import load_iris

from sklearn.model_selection import train_test_split

from sklearn.preprocessing import StandardScaler


# Load sample dataset (Iris dataset)

data = load_iris()

X, y = data.data, data.target


# Split the data into training and testing sets

X_train, X_test, y_train, y_test = train_test_split(X, y, test_size=0.2, random_state=42)
```

```python
# Standardize the features

scaler = StandardScaler()

X_train = scaler.fit_transform(X_train)

X_test = scaler.transform(X_test)
```

b. Supervised Learning - Classification:

Scikit-learn provides numerous classifiers for classification tasks. Here's an example using the k-nearest neighbors (KNN) classifier:

```python
from sklearn.neighbors import KNeighborsClassifier

from sklearn.metrics import accuracy_score


# Create and train the classifier
```

```python
knn = KNeighborsClassifier(n_neighbors=3)
knn.fit(X_train, y_train)

# Make predictions on the test set
y_pred = knn.predict(X_test)

# Evaluate the classifier's accuracy
accuracy = accuracy_score(y_test, y_pred)
print("Accuracy:", accuracy)
```

c. Supervised Learning - Regression:

For regression tasks, scikit-learn offers various regression models. Here's an example using linear regression:

```python
from sklearn.linear_model import LinearRegression

from sklearn.metrics import mean_squared_error


# Create and train the regression model

reg = LinearRegression()

reg.fit(X_train, y_train)


# Make predictions on the test set

y_pred = reg.predict(X_test)


# Evaluate the regression model's performance using Mean Squared Error (MSE)

mse = mean_squared_error(y_test, y_pred)

print("Mean Squared Error:", mse)
```

d. Unsupervised Learning - Clustering:

Scikit-learn provides clustering algorithms for unsupervised learning tasks. Here's an example using K-means clustering:

```python
from sklearn.cluster import KMeans
from sklearn.metrics import silhouette_score

# Create and train the K-means clustering model
kmeans = KMeans(n_clusters=3)
kmeans.fit(X_train)

# Make predictions on the test set
y_pred = kmeans.predict(X_test)
```

```
# Evaluate the clustering model using Silhouette
Score

silhouette_avg = silhouette_score(X_test, y_pred)

print("Silhouette Score:", silhouette_avg)
```

4. Model Selection and Evaluation:

Scikit-learn includes various tools for model
selection and evaluation, such as cross-validation,
grid search for hyperparameter tuning, and
performance metrics.

```python
from sklearn.model_selection import
cross_val_score, GridSearchCV
```

```
# Cross-validation for model evaluation

cv_scores = cross_val_score(knn, X_train, y_train,
cv=5)

print("Cross-Validation Scores:", cv_scores)


# Hyperparameter tuning using Grid Search

param_grid = {'n_neighbors': [1, 3, 5, 7, 9]}

grid_search = GridSearchCV(knn, param_grid,
cv=5)

grid_search.fit(X_train, y_train)


best_params = grid_search.best_params_

print("Best Parameters:", best_params)
```
```

Scikit-learn offers many more functionalities for various machine learning tasks, including dimensionality reduction, feature selection, model persistence, and more. With its comprehensive
```

documentation and user-friendly API, scikit-learn is an excellent library for getting started with machine learning in Python.

Conclusion:

Throughout this Python journey, we've covered a wide range of topics and gained valuable knowledge in various areas. Let's summarize the key points and concepts we've explored:

1. **Basics of Python**: We started with the fundamentals of Python, learning about variables,

data types, operators, and control flow constructs like loops and conditional statements.

2. **Functions and Modules**: We delved into defining functions, understanding scope, and organizing code into modules for better reusability.

3. **File Handling**: We explored reading and writing files, including text and binary files, and learned about handling exceptions during file operations.

4. **Python Libraries**: We discussed essential Python libraries like NumPy, Pandas, and Matplotlib. NumPy for numerical operations and arrays, Pandas for data manipulation and analysis, and Matplotlib for data visualization.

5. **Object-Oriented Programming (OOP)**: We explored OOP principles, classes, objects, and inheritance, enabling us to write more organized and reusable code.

6. **Web Development**: We introduced web frameworks like Django and Flask and learned how to create simple web applications using Python.

7. **Data Analysis with NumPy and Pandas**: We covered data analysis using NumPy and Pandas, including handling data types, filtering, grouping, and aggregating data.

8. **Machine Learning with Scikit-learn**: We explored basic machine learning tasks with Scikit-learn, such as data preprocessing, supervised learning (classification and regression), and unsupervised learning (clustering).

9. **Database Interaction**: We discussed connecting to databases like SQLite, MySQL, and PostgreSQL, executing SQL queries, and managing data.

10. **Artificial Intelligence and Natural Language Processing**: We touched on AI concepts, including machine learning, NLP, computer vision, and robotics.

Throughout this journey, we've seen how Python's versatility and extensive libraries make it a powerful language for various tasks, from simple scripting to complex data analysis and machine learning projects. We've gained practical knowledge in Python programming, data manipulation, web development, and machine learning, equipping us with the skills to tackle real-world challenges using Python.

Remember that programming is an ongoing journey of learning and exploration. Continue building on the knowledge gained here, exploring new topics, and applying Python in various domains to grow your expertise further. Happy coding!

Congratulations on completing this Python journey! You've taken significant strides in learning a versatile and powerful programming language.

However, this is just the beginning of an exciting and rewarding journey with Python.

Python's applications are vast and diverse, making it an indispensable tool across various domains. Here are some encouraging words to continue your learning and explore Python's diverse applications:

1. **Explore New Domains**: Python's flexibility allows you to delve into various fields like data science, web development, artificial intelligence, automation, game development, and more. Don't be afraid to step into new territories and apply Python to solve unique challenges.

2. **Work on Real Projects**: Learning is most effective when put into practice. Start working on real projects that interest you. Whether it's building a web application, analyzing datasets, or creating a machine learning model, hands-on experience will deepen your understanding and boost your skills.

3. **Contribute to Open Source**: Join the vibrant Python community by contributing to open-source projects. It's a fantastic way to learn from experienced developers, collaborate with others, and make a positive impact on the wider Python ecosystem.

4. **Stay Updated**: Python is an evolving language with new features and libraries being developed regularly. Stay up-to-date with the latest trends, releases, and best practices by reading blogs, attending conferences, and following Python experts.

5. **Online Courses and Tutorials**: Continue learning through online courses, tutorials, and documentation. Many platforms offer advanced Python courses on specific topics, allowing you to deepen your knowledge in areas of interest.

6. **Network and Connect**: Engage with other Python enthusiasts, join forums, and participate in Python meetups or conferences. Networking

provides opportunities to learn from others, collaborate on projects, and find mentors.

7. **Embrace Challenges**: Programming can be challenging, but remember that every obstacle is an opportunity to learn and grow. Embrace challenges with a positive mindset and persist through difficult problems.

8. **Share Your Knowledge**: Teach others what you've learned. Sharing your knowledge not only solidifies your understanding but also contributes to the Python community's growth.

Remember, Python is a tool that empowers your creativity. There's no limit to what you can achieve with it. So, continue your learning journey, explore Python's vast applications, and turn your ideas into reality. The Python community is a supportive and welcoming space, and you'll find endless possibilities awaiting you. Happy coding, and keep exploring!

Appendix:

1. **Python**: A high-level, interpreted programming language known for its simplicity, readability, and versatility.

2. **Interpreter**: A program that reads and executes Python code line by line.

3. **Variable**: A named container that holds a value or data.

4. **Data Type**: Defines the type of data that a variable can hold, such as integers, floats, strings, lists, tuples, dictionaries, etc.

5. **Function**: A reusable block of code that performs a specific task and can take inputs and return outputs.

6. **Module**: A Python file containing code and definitions that can be reused in other Python programs.

7. **List**: A mutable and ordered collection of elements, enclosed in square brackets.

8. **Tuple**: An immutable and ordered collection of elements, enclosed in parentheses.

9. **Dictionary**: A collection of key-value pairs, enclosed in curly braces, where keys are unique and used to access values.

10. **String**: A sequence of characters, enclosed in single or double quotes.

11. **Control Flow**: The order in which statements and blocks of code are executed in a program, controlled by conditionals and loops.

12. **Conditional Statements**: Used to make decisions in code using if, else, and elif.

13. **Loop**: A structure used to repeat a set of statements multiple times, such as for loop and while loop.

14. **Exception**: An error that occurs during program execution, which can be caught and handled using try-except blocks.

15. **Object-Oriented Programming (OOP)**: A programming paradigm that uses objects and classes to organize and structure code.

16. **Class**: A blueprint for creating objects with properties and methods.

17. **Object**: An instance of a class, representing a real-world entity with its attributes and behaviors.

18. **Inheritance**: A mechanism in OOP where a class can inherit properties and methods from another class.

19. **Package**: A collection of Python modules and subpackages, providing a hierarchical organization of code.

20. **NumPy**: A library for numerical computing in Python, providing support for arrays and mathematical operations.

21. **Pandas**: A library for data manipulation and analysis, offering powerful data structures like DataFrames and Series.

22. **Matplotlib**: A library for creating various types of plots and data visualizations.

23. **Machine Learning**: A subset of artificial intelligence, focusing on algorithms that enable computers to learn patterns from data.

24. **Scikit-learn**: A popular machine learning library in Python, providing tools for various machine learning tasks.

25. **TensorFlow**: An open-source deep learning library developed by Google, known for its flexibility and scalability.

26. **Keras**: A user-friendly deep learning library built on top of TensorFlow.

27. **SQLite**: A lightweight, serverless, and self-contained relational database engine.

28. **MySQL**: A popular open-source relational database management system.

29. **PostgreSQL**: An open-source object-relational database management system.

30. **API**: Application Programming Interface, a set of rules and protocols that allows different software applications to communicate with each other.

www.ingramcontent.com/pod-product-compliance
Lightning Source LLC
Chambersburg PA
CBHW072155290526
45794CB00004B/1520